LET'S EXPLORE LIFE SCIENCE

Exploring
FOOD CHAINS and FOOD WEBS

Ella Hawley

PowerKiDS press.

New York

Published in 2013 by The Rosen Publishing Group, Inc.
29 East 21st Street, New York, NY 10010

First Edition

Editor: Jennifer Way
Book Design: Kate Laczynski

Photo Credits: Cover (main), pp. 5 (butterfly, coyote, sunflower, vulture), 6–7, 7 (main), 8, 11 (top, bottom), 13, 14, 15 (top, bottom), 16–17, 17 (main), 21 (all images), 22 Shutterstock.com; cover (owl), pp. 5 (prairie dog), 12 iStockphoto/Thinkstock; cover (lizard), p. 19 (snail, fish) PhotoDisc; p. 4 © www.iStockphoto.com/fotolinchen; p. 5 (bullfrog) © www.iStockphoto.com/Bruce MacQueen; p. 5 (prairie grass) © www.iStockphoto.com/kokophoto; p. 9 by Kate Laczynski; p. 10 Anup Shah/Photodisc/Thinkstock; p. 19 (egret) © www.iStockphoto.com/Alicia Pastiran; p. 19 (dragonfly, mosquito) © www.iStockphoto.com/Antagain; p. 19 (frog) © www.iStockphoto.com/Jens Gade; p. 19 (kingfisher) © www.iStockphoto.com/Inge Schepers; p. 19 (pond plants) © www.iStockphoto.com/Yusuf Anil Akduygu; p. 20 Jupiterimages/Comstock/Thinkstock.

Library of Congress Cataloging-in-Publication Data

Hawley, Ella.
  Exploring food chains and food webs / by Ella Hawley. — 1st ed.
     p. cm. — (Let's explore life science)
  Includes index.
  ISBN 978-1-4488-6173-6 (library binding) — ISBN 978-1-4488-6304-4 (pbk.) — ISBN 978-1-4488-6305-1 (6-pack)
  1. Food chains (Ecology)—Juvenile literature. I. Title.
  QH541.14.H39 2013
  577'.16—dc23
                                        2011019502

Manufactured in the United States of America

CPSIA Compliance Information: Batch #SW12PK: For Further Information contact Rosen Publishing, New York, New York at 1-800-237-9932

CONTENTS

It's All Connected

Prairie dogs eat grasses and other leafy plants.

Did you know that all the plants and animals in the world are linked together? For example, a blade of grass grows and is eaten by a prairie dog, which in turn is eaten by a coyote. This connection between plants and animals is called a food chain.

Most animals do not eat only one thing. These animals belong to more than one food chain. A group of food chains is called a food web. A food web shows you all the different relationships plants and animals have to one another. This book will show you the different roles living organisms play in Earth's food chains and food webs.

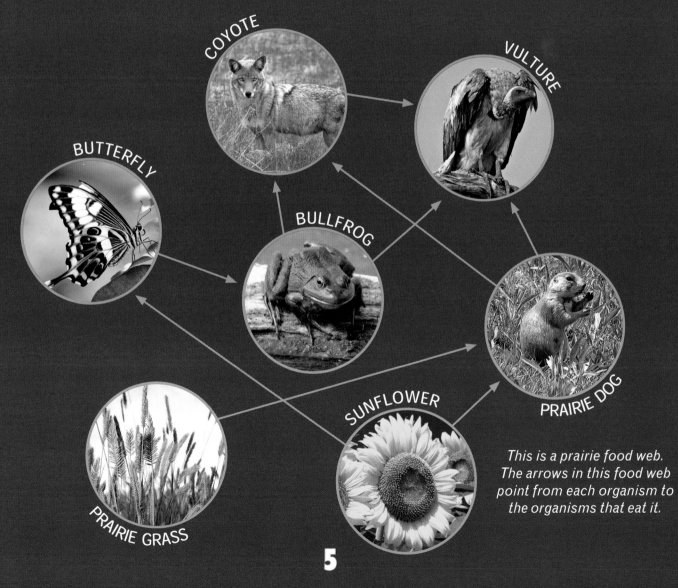

COYOTE

VULTURE

BUTTERFLY

BULLFROG

PRAIRIE DOG

SUNFLOWER

PRAIRIE GRASS

This is a prairie food web. The arrows in this food web point from each organism to the organisms that eat it.

It Starts with Plants

There are around 400,000 different kinds of plants in the world, and those are just the ones we know about! Many animals, from butterflies to fruit bats to cows, count on plants for the food they need to live. In fact, every food chain and food web starts with plants.

Plants like these sunflowers use energy from the Sun to make their own food. Chlorophyll is what gives the leaves their green color.

Plants are called the producers in a food chain. This is because they produce their own food through **photosynthesis**. A chemical in plants called **chlorophyll** lets them make their own food. Chlorophyll takes in the energy from sunlight. Using that energy, along with water and a gas called carbon dioxide the plant makes the sugars that are its food.

Butterflies drink the sweet liquid in flowers called nectar.

Let Them Eat Plants!

Okapis have long, dark-colored tongues they use to pull leaves off trees. They are related to giraffes.

Most living things cannot make food inside themselves, as plants can. Instead, they must find things to eat. Some animals eat only plants. These animals are called **herbivores**. Koalas, bees, and giant pandas are all herbivores. Herbivores are called primary consumers in the food chain. Primary consumers eat and get their energy from plants, which get their energy from the Sun.

Okapis are herbivores that live in the Ituri Forest, in central Africa. They move slowly through the thick rain forest looking for leaves, twigs, and fruits to eat. These animals eat up to 65 pounds (29 kg) of plant matter each day!

Koalas are herbivores that eat mostly leaves from eucalyptus trees.

On the Hunt

Lions live in the savannas of Africa. They eat large mammals such as zebras.

Herbivores are not the only hungry animals around. **Carnivores** are animals that eat other animals. These hunters include lions, sharks, hawks, and wolves. Carnivores that eat herbivores are secondary consumers. Carnivores that eat other carnivores are tertiary consumers. Carnivores that are not normally eaten by any other carnivores are at the top of their food chains. They are **apex predators**.

Gray wolves hunt in packs. They eat plant eaters, such as elk, moose, and caribou. They also eat smaller animals, such as rabbits. Wolves, and other carnivores, generally have great senses, which help them hunt. They also have sharp teeth and claws to help them kill their **prey**.

Great white sharks are apex predators in their ocean habitat.

Gray wolves use their strong senses of smell and hearing to help them find prey.

Having It All

Raccoons eat just about anything. Raccoons that live near people often dig through garbage cans to look for food.

What about animals that sometimes eat plants and sometimes eat meat? These animals are called **omnivores** because they eat a bit of everything! Bears, people, and raccoons are a few examples of omnivores. Omnivores are secondary consumers.

Meerkats are omnivores that live in the deserts and **savannas** of southern Africa. They eat scorpions, lizards, insects, birds, fruits, and the roots of many desert plants. They live in large groups and are known for standing on their back legs as they watch for danger. Many animals are happy to make a meal out of meerkats, including hawks and jackals. Meerkats are just one link in the savanna's food chain.

Members of meerkat groups take turns keeping a lookout for predators.

Scavengers and Parasites

The bluestreak cleaner wrasse shown here is eating the parasites off of the skin of a moray eel.

Nothing in nature is wasted. There is always a plant or animal willing to take energy from the leftovers another living thing has left behind. Some carnivores and omnivores are **scavengers**. They eat sick or dying animals and dead animals that other animals have killed.

Parasites are another part of the food chain. They live on a host and get **nutrients** from it without giving the host anything in return. Yet even parasites provide food for other animals. In the ocean, fish called cleaners eat parasites from the skin of other fish. In the rain forest, monkeys groom each other and make a meal out of each other's parasites.

Vultures (right) and hyenas (below) are both scavengers. Hyenas sometimes hunt prey, while vultures tend to kill only sick or dying animals.

Decomposers

Earthworms eat dead plant and animal matter. As they move through the soil, they break it up and pass nutrients back into the soil through their waste.

Often the last links in any food chain or web are the **decomposers**. Decomposers break down dead plant and animal matter. Worms, fungi, and bacteria are decomposers. Fungi include mushrooms, molds, and mildew. Bacteria are tiny living things that can be found everywhere. Some help animals **digest** food. Others break down wastes from animals. Still others turn milk into cheese or yogurt.

When decomposers break down plants and animals, the nutrients from these things go into the soil. This makes the soil richer and lets more plants grow in it. Soon animals will eat these new plants and the food chain begins again.

Mushrooms are decomposers that feed on dead plant matter such as this tree.

A Closer Look: A Pond Food Web

Let's take a closer look at a food web that could be found in a pond habitat. Plants such as pondweed and reeds grow in the pond. Snails eat small plants in the water. Kingfishers fly to the pond to eat the snails, as well as insects. Some of these insects also eat the plants in the pond.

Frogs eat insects, too. An egret, in turn, may eat frogs. Egrets also eat other pond animals, such as small fish, which may eat other fish, insects, or plants in the pond. All the living organisms in this pond habitat overlap to form a food web.

GRAPHIC ORGANIZER: Food Web

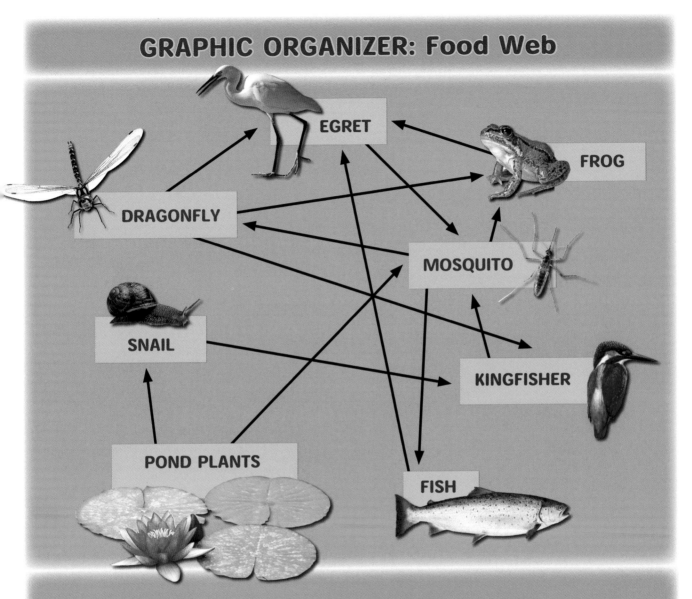

This food web shows the relationships between different organisms in a pond habitat. Mosquitoes eat the nectar of pond plants. They also eat the blood of warm-blooded animals, such as the egret.

Habitats Are Everywhere

The plants and animals that live in a place make up a habitat. Deserts, grasslands, forests, and swamps are all different kinds of habitats. Each habitat has its own food chains that depend on the plants and animals that live there. A shark is not part of the food chain in a desert habitat, but it is a big part of the food webs in the oceans where it lives.

What kinds of habitats are there in your town? Did you know your backyard and the park near your home are both habitats? What plants and animals make up their food chains?

The Everglades, in Florida, has swamp habitats, which have many different food chains and food webs.

A SWAMP FOOD CHAIN

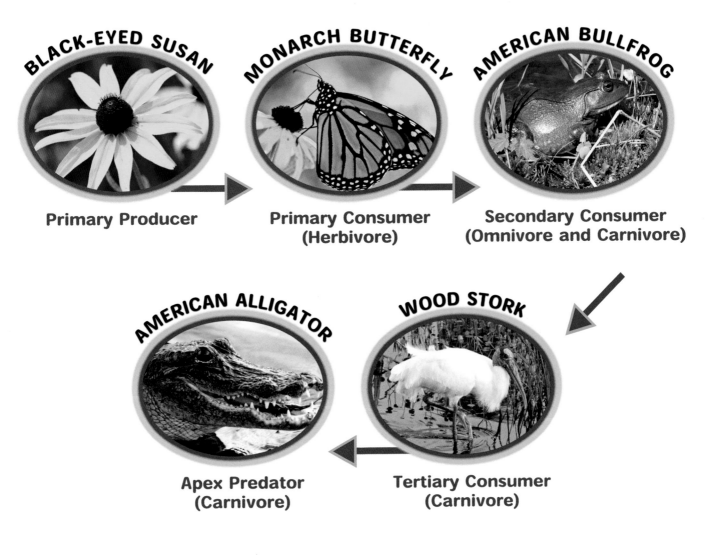

BLACK-EYED SUSAN
Primary Producer

MONARCH BUTTERFLY
Primary Consumer
(Herbivore)

AMERICAN BULLFROG
Secondary Consumer
(Omnivore and Carnivore)

AMERICAN ALLIGATOR
Apex Predator
(Carnivore)

WOOD STORK
Tertiary Consumer
(Carnivore)

A Delicate Balance

Food chains and food webs are healthy if they are balanced. If something happens to one of the parts, then the whole chain or web is affected.

What might happen if a lot of **fertilizer** gets into a pond? The fertilizer may make lots of **algae** grow. The extra algae may

> If there are changes in the amount of algae in this pond, it can affect everything in a food chain, not just the living organisms that eat it.

make the water unhealthy for the fish living there and they die. The raccoons that eat the fish do not have enough food. They either die or move elsewhere. The coyotes that counted on those animals for food might die or move, too. Each food chain or web has a delicate balance. That is why it is important to keep the different parts of each habitat healthy.

GLOSSARY

algae (AL-jee) Plantlike living things without roots or stems that live in water.

apex predators (AY-peks PREH-duh-terz) Predators that are at the top of their food chains.

carnivores (KAHR-neh-vorz) Animals that eat only other animals.

chlorophyll (KLOR-uh-fil) Green matter inside plants that allows them to use energy from sunlight to make their own food.

decomposers (dee-kum-POH-zerz) Living things that break down the cells of dead plants and animals into simpler parts.

digest (dy-JEST) To break down food so that the body can use it.

fertilizer (FUR-tuh-lyz-er) Something put in soil to help crops grow.

herbivores (ER-buh-vorz) Animals that eat only plants.

nutrients (NOO-tree-ents) Food that a living thing needs to live and grow.

omnivores (OM-nih-vawrz) Animals that eat both plants and animals.

parasites (PER-uh-syts) Living things that live in, on, or with other living things.

photosynthesis (foh-toh-SIN-thuh-sus) The way in which green plants make their own food from sunlight, water, and a gas called carbon dioxide.

prey (PRAY) An animal that is hunted by another animal for food.

savannas (suh-VA-nuz) Grasslands with few trees or bushes.

scavengers (SKA-ven-jurz) Animals that eat dead things.

INDEX

WEB SITES

Due to the changing nature of Internet links, PowerKids
Press has developed an online list of Web sites related
to the subject of this book. This site is updated regularly.
Please use this link to access the list:
www.powerkidslinks.com/lels/chains/